MODERN**BLUES** **GUITAR**SOLOING

Master The Art of Modern Blues-Rock Guitar in 100 Killer Licks

JOSH**SMITH**

FUNDAMENTAL**CHANGES**

Modern Blues Guitar Soloing

Master The Art of Modern Blues-Rock Guitar in 100 Killer Licks

ISBN: 978-1-78933-389-3

Published by www.fundamental-changes.com

www.fundamental-changes.com

Over 12,000 fans on Facebook: **FundamentalChangesInGuitar**

Instagram: **FundamentalChanges**

For over 350 Free Guitar Lessons with Videos Check Out

www.fundamental-changes.com

Cover Image Copyright: Author photo by McKenzie Lenora, used by permission.

https://www.instagram.com/mackenzielenoraphotography/

All audio tracks created and recorded by Josh Smith at Flat V Studios, Los Angeles. With special thanks to Travis Carlton (bass) and Lemar Carter (drums).

https://www.joshsmithguitar.com/flat-v

Contents

About the Author...4

Preface 5

Introduction 6

Get the Audio 8

Chapter One – Blues Shuffle 9

Chapter Two – Funky Blues 24

Chapter Three – Jump Blues 41

Chapter Four – Slow Blues Ballad 63

Chapter Five – Classic Rock Blues 76

Conclusion 90

About the Author

Blues-rock guitar virtuoso, singer-songwriter and producer, Josh Smith, is hailed the world over as a master guitarist with raw talent and power to spare. Blending his signature mix of blues, rock, jazz and country into dynamic original songs, Smith is known for his incendiary live performances, whether at the Grammy Awards or the Kennedy Center Honors with Mick Jagger, Raphael Saadiq and others.

Along with touring the world, recording and performing with renowned artists such as Joe Bonamassa, Eric Johnson, Andy Timmons, Kirk Fletcher and others, Smith is also a producer and owns Flat V Studios in Los Angeles. He has produced artists including Reese Wynans (*Sweet Release*), Eric Gales (*Crown*), Joanna Conner (*4801 South Indiana Avenue*), Joanne Shaw Taylor (*The Blues Album*), Andy Timmons (*Electric Truth*), Jimmy Hall, Larry Mccray (*Blues Without You*), Artur Menezes (winner of the Eric Clapton 2019 Crossroads Festival; *Anyday, Anytime* and *Fading Away*), Seth Rosenbloom (*Keep on Turning*), Jamey Arent (*The Back Burner*) and many more.

Josh lives in Los Angeles with his wife and son and is currently touring with Joe Bonamassa.

"Josh is one of my favorite musicians on the planet. His musical depth and guitar playing transcend the boundaries of the blues genre into a genre of his own. I am always proud to share a stage with him and even prouder to call him my friend."

–Joe Bonamassa

"As a player, writer, singer and producer, Josh Smith has it all. Smith can truly rock. But his sense is strengthened by tasteful ideas, substantive playing, and a deep understanding of blues guitar."

–Vintage Guitar Magazine

Preface

I want to thank you for picking up this book, and for your interest in what I do. The fact that anyone cares enough about my guitar playing and music to want to purchase a book about it is an amazing honor, and one that is not lost on me. When the idea for this book was presented to me, I knew exactly what I wanted it to be: an entryway into all things me is, I guess, the best way to explain it.

I treat the blues, guitar playing and improvisation seriously, and I wanted to give readers a doorway into my approach to all those things. The goal here should be to take the overall concepts and fundamental ideas and apply them to your voice, your world, your playing. Sure, it's cool to learn some new lines, but if you can learn a new concept and add a new approach to your playing – that will last forever.

I hope you find that inspiration in this book. I hope it knocks down a few walls for you. And more than anything, I hope it just makes you excited to pick up your guitar and play!

Thanks to Tim, Joseph and their team at Fundamental Changes for putting this together!

Josh Smith

Los Angeles

Introduction

The aim of this book

This book is organized around a range of musical "situations" that the modern blues guitarist is likely to encounter. There are lots of different takes on the blues, but the following five situations cover a wide range of modern blues vocabulary. In turn we'll look at:

- The classic blues shuffle

- Funky blues

- Swinging "jump" blues

- A blues ballad

- Classic rock blues

Each tune is played in a different, common blues key. In each chapter, we'll look at the kind of blues language that is appropriate for each style and break down the melodic ideas into lines that work over four bar sections of the blues:

- The I chord

- The IV chord, transitioning back to the I chord

- The V to I chord turnaround

My goal is to grow your blues vocabulary, add some new ideas and equip you with an arsenal of solid licks that work over each chord of the blues.

During my late teens and early twenties, I gigged relentlessly, playing around 300 shows per year in small clubs across the States. While that didn't make me rich, it refined my playing and distilled my ideas down to what *really works*. The process of playing live helps to dispense with throwaway, average ideas and focus on the good stuff – the licks that get a reaction from the audience. I want to pass onto you the blues vocabulary that stood the test of many tough audiences and survived!

As we look at the ideas I played when soloing over these five tracks, I'll explain both the techniques being used and the musical thinking behind the lines. But before we dive in, I want to give you an overview of the musical "tools" you'll be using as you learn these licks. When analyzing my own playing (which is a melting pot of all my musical influences over the years), these are the ideas that I most often turn to.

Tools of the Modern Blues Player

1. Feel and phrasing. If you want to get a visceral reaction from an audience, the bottom line is that you have to make your guitar sing. This can be a matter of feel and dynamics, but also comes down to phrasing. You'll see in the solos that follow that sometimes I purposely limit myself to a small area of the neck – using maybe just three strings in a four-fret zone, for instance, or perhaps just the top two strings. The aim of this is to squeeze as much creative expression as I can out of that limited space. It makes me work harder to come up with the good stuff. I also aim to use vocal phrasing – lines that mimic the human voice and inject soul into the music.

2. Storytelling devices. Every solo should tell a story, not just be a collection of random licks strung together. To do that we can use the classic blues device of call and response phrasing, which gives a solo a sense of continuity. We can also use repetition (the same lick will sound totally fresh with different dynamics and articulation or played different beats of the bar). And, most importantly, we can use the idea of developing themes that carry through a solo, gluing it together.

3. Country-Jazz influenced licks. You'll hear some country and jazz influence in my playing. Although the blues is at the heart of who I am as a musician, I was influenced early on by players like Danny Gatton. What Danny could do over simple country chord changes blew me away and changed my picking style overnight. I was also drawn to the ideas of jazz as a way of spicing up my blues playing and finding my own voice. We'll explore my use of hybrid picking and also jazz-style chromatic approach notes in the material that follows.

4. Rhythmic variation. Lastly, we'll also look at devices such as playing triplets over straight 4/4 grooves to break up the rhythm, playing lines organized into odd note groupings, using pedal tones, and we'll learn how to apply hybrid picking to play licks that would otherwise be extremely difficult to pull off. We'll also discuss how to play lines that move *through*, rather than over the changes, crossing the bar line with rhythm and phrasing that make them more exciting and less predictable.

How to Use This Book

Mastering any style of music is like learning a language. Over the years, I've listened to lots of different players who have influenced me, and I've absorbed something from each one. But while those influences enriched and contributed to my playing in different ways, the end goal was always to develop my own style.

I suggest you do the same. There will be ideas here that you've not thought of playing before, and I hope they inspire you. By all means learn them note-for-note and add them to your musical vocabulary, but it's more important that you make them your own. When you hear an idea you really like, grab it and work with it. You don't have to play it exactly like me because you can play it like *you*.

Then, experiment… transpose that lick to different keys and up/down octaves; play it beginning on different beats of the bar; try it over different chords in the blues to see what effect that has. This is the way to absorb new ideas into your playing.

Above all, relax, have fun, and enjoy playing over the backing tracks I created in the studio, which you have access to as part of the audio download for this book. Find out how to get them on the next page.

See you on the road!

Josh.

Get the Audio

The audio files for this book are available to download for free from **www.fundamental-changes.com.** The link is in the top right-hand corner. Click on the "Guitar" link then simply select this book title from the drop-down menu and follow the instructions to get the audio.

We recommend that you download the files directly to your computer, not to your tablet, and extract them there before adding them to your media library. You can then put them onto your tablet, iPod or burn them to CD. On the download page there are instructions and we also provide technical support via the contact form.

For over 350 free guitar lessons with videos check out:

www.fundamental-changes.com

Join our free Facebook Community of Cool Musicians

www.facebook.com/groups/fundamentalguitar

Tag us for a share on Instagram: **FundamentalChanges**

Chapter One – Blues Shuffle

As a guitar player, the blues is at the heart of everything I play. I grew up with this music and it's the music I love. Even if I'm playing something that has more of a jazz, country or soul feel, the blues is always there, because it's the core of who I am and what I play.

On one level, part of me thinks that you can't *teach* the blues, you just have to *feel* it! But the truth is, the more you learn about the blues, and the more you play it, the more you absorb the music and really begin to feel it. Here, you'll learn a whole range of blues vocabulary that will help you to get inside the music, understand it, and express yourself through it. Before long, you'll begin to develop your own voice and put your own unique spin on the music.

As you work on your time, phrasing and technique to play the licks here, remember that the end goal is to express yourself with *feeling*. We can have all the technique in the world and still fail to move an audience or connect emotionally with people. As a musician, I self-edit all the time. I hear lots of musical ideas in my head – sometimes sophisticated harmonic ideas or advanced techniques that I *could* use at a given moment – but the stuff I choose to let out is always what I feel is the most honest in any situation. If you think of all your favorite players and what you love about them, it nearly always comes down to their ability to convey an emotion that you can identify with. They make you *feel something.* And that's the ultimate goal, to help you become a player who is well-schooled, but who plays with authenticity, confidence and commitment.

Let's get started!

The Blues Shuffle

The shuffle is one of the most important grooves you'll encounter in the blues. Although it has many variations, and will sound a little different when played by musicians from the Mississippi Delta to Chicago to Texas, it always has that driving, dotted 1/8th note feel that swings hard and really captures the attitude of the blues.

Shuffles can be fast or slow (check out Stevie Ray Vaughan's *Pride and Joy* for a great example of a slower shuffle) and are often driven by chugging chords or single-note riffs. In this chapter, our workhorse tune is a 12-bar shuffle in the key of Bb, played at 127 beats per minute (bpm).

We're going to break down the structure of this blues into four-bar chunks and look at some of the vocabulary I play over the different sections. Working in four-bar sections means you'll learn lines to play over:

- The I chord (Bb) to the IV chord (Eb) and back

- The IV chord (Eb) and the transition back to the I chord

- The turnaround section where the V chord (F7) resolves back to the I chord

Although each example has been transcribed as a standalone lick, if you group together every three examples and play them in order, they'll form a complete solo over one chorus of the blues.

Also, remember the approaches and melodic ideas I talked about in the introduction. As we work through the chapter, I'll point out these ideas and explain any special techniques needed to play the licks smoothly.

After you've learned the series of licks, at the end of the chapter there is a complete solo for you to learn spanning two choruses.

It's important to make a strong opening statement to any solo, so here's a lick to get us started. It uses a pickup triplet phrase to hit the bend in bar one, then leaves some space. In bar two, the phrase over the IV chord (Eb) uses the notes of the Bb Blues scale (Bb Db Eb E F A). In bar four, I switch to Bb Minor Pentatonic (Bb Db Eb F Ab) to begin a phrase that will dovetail with Example 1b.

Example 1a

When navigating the changes of the blues, the aim is to play *through* rather than *over* the changes. When the chord changes, it sticks out like a sore thumb if we're thinking, "OK, the chord's changed, so now I need to play a I chord lick." Instead, we need to be constantly aware of what the harmony is doing and signal that to the listener by playing lines that flow from one chord into the next.

In bar two of this example, the Bb chord of bar three is anticipated by a lick that highlights its major 3rd interval, signaling what's coming next. Similarly, at the end of bar four, a chromatic run down targets the C note on beat 1 of bar five, which is the 5th of the F7 chord.

Example 1b

Example 1c starts with the chromatic run down from the end of the previous example to make a complete lick. Bar three is a well-known blues phrase, but with 1/8th and 1/16th note triplet articulation to change it up. Listen to the audio example to get it right, as it's all about the feel.

Example 1c

One thing you may notice about my playing is that I play lots of phrases that cross the bar line. In the example below, a pickup phrase introduces the bend up to the D note in bar one (the 3rd of Bb7). After hitting that note, I leave some space, then the last note of bar one begins a phrase that happens over the Eb7 chord. Anticipating the chords makes it feel like each lick has a destination and purpose.

Example 1d

Notice that at the beginning of the previous example and this next one, I'm working in one small zone of the fretboard and only using the top two strings. Remember the tools mentioned in the introduction? At times I deliberately restrict myself to a limited area of the neck. The reason for doing so is twofold: it gives the licks a sense of continuity, because they have the same timbre, but more importantly it forces me to get creative. I need to avoid playing an identical phrase, change up the articulation, make each idea stand out... It's a great discipline to refine your phrasing and work on your feel.

In bar five of this lick, I play an idea often used in jazz, which is to *imply* a chord change. The idea is that you spell out a chord that could be used to enrich the harmony, even though it's not written on the lead sheet. A jazz blues will typically have many more chord changes than a standard blues, and in bar five here, the chord would usually be G7 in a Bb jazz blues. On the backing track, the bass player is playing a walking pattern rather than resting on one note, so that allows me to play a lick that implies the underlying chord is G7 rather than Bb. This idea continues in Example 1f.

Example 1e

In a jazz blues, the G7 chord will often be followed by a Cm7, which leads to F7 (a ii V movement), before returning to the I chord (Bb). The quick ascending run in the pickup bar of this example implies the Cm7 sound. The simple, three-chord foundation of the blues makes it the ideal vehicle to work ideas like this into your playing. Notice the use of 1/8th note triplets throughout, which help to make the line swing.

Example 1f

Another useful way of limiting what you play to inspire creativity is to say to yourself, whatever lick I play first, *that* is the theme for my solo.

Try spontaneously playing a lick right now, without thinking too much about it. That's your theme! Everything you play for the rest of your solo should build on or answer that statement. You can develop it, change it up, build on it, move it to different places in the bar… but work with *that* theme. You'll find your solo begins to tell a story.

Here's my take on this idea. In bar one I played a spontaneous lick on the top three strings beginning with a *blues curl*. This means applying a slight bend to the note. It's not even a half step, so is usually notated as a quarter bend (as below). This, and the couple of notes that follow it, is my theme. Let's see where it goes over the next three examples, which you can combine to play a full chorus solo.

First, I repeat the theme straight away because it has a different effect over the Eb chord in bar two. I play it again in bar three, where I build on the idea. I allow the line to take a different shape in bar four, but return to those two supporting notes at the end.

Example 1g

In the next example I move away from the theme a little in bar one, but hint at it again in bar two. Overall, this lick has a question and answer format. Bars 1-2 are the question and bars 3-4 form the response.

Example 1h

For the final example of this set of three, I work my way back into the zone of the neck where the theme began. The line goes in a different direction and I play some new ideas, but I return to the theme in bar four. Have a close listen to the audio before playing this example to get the articulation and rhythmic phrasing down.

Example 1i

Here's another theme-driven lick. This time I play a motif based around the Bb root note on the second string, 11th fret. Throughout the lick I keep returning to that Bb and it acts as an anchor for everything that happens around it. It's a simple but effective strategy for creating a line that has a sense of continuity.

Example 1j

In the next example I keep the Bb note theme going for a while longer before allowing myself to break out of it in the latter half of bar three and bar four.

Example 1k

For the turnaround part of the lick I'm exploring a new idea. To outline the sound of the F7 chord in bars 1-2, I'm using the F Mixolydian scale (F G A Bb C D Eb). This the fifth mode of Bb Major and like playing a Bb Major scale beginning and ending on an F note (though it's better to think of F Mixolydian as a scale and more importantly a *sound* in its own right).

I've also included in this line another idea borrowed from jazz, which is to add chromatic passing notes between some of the scale tones. Sometimes we want to play a line that weaves around the harmony in a less obvious way. Chromatic tones (notes that don't belong to the parent key) can be used to "target" scale or chord tones.

In simple terms, we have a target in mind (in bar one it's the A note on the second string, 10th fret that falls on the "3&" of the beat) and we approach that target from above or below with a chromatic note.

The phrase in the middle of bar one is known as an "enclosure" in jazz because we play a scale tone above the target (Bb, second string, fret 11), then a scale tone below (G, second string, fret 8), then a chromatic approach note (Ab, second string, fret 9) before hitting the target note (the A note on the 10th fret, the 3rd of the F7 chord).

Play just those four notes in isolation and you've got a staple bebop phrase used by everyone from Charlie Parker onwards.

Example 1l

The next example has an immediate call and response idea in bars 1-3. Often call and response licks take place over a longer number of bars, but this lick immediately answers the first phrase with a second, then alternates between the two phrases.

Bars 4-5 have a faster 1/16th note lick for you to learn. Watch out for the timing in bar four – sometimes I like to "interrupt" a 1/16th note run with an 1/8th note to break up the rhythm. Play through the line slowly to begin with and work out a comfortable, economic fingering before bringing it up to tempo.

The notes come from a hybrid pentatonic scale. I'm blending together both Bb Major and Bb Minor Pentatonic scales. Because blues chords are frequently played as dominant 7s, it's fine to blur the lines between major and minor tonalities when soloing over them.

Example 1m

For the next four-bar section, here's another jazz-influenced idea. In bar one, the notes for the lick come from the Eb Mixolydian scale (Eb F G Ab Bb C Db). Even though Eb is the IV chord in the overall key of Bb, because blues chords are played as dominant 7s we can treat *every* chord in the blues as though it's a V chord. Pause and think about this idea for a second and let that information sink in.

Eb Mixolydian fits perfectly over Eb7, which at this moment in time is functioning like the V chord in the key of Ab Major. It's like we're taking a quick snapshot of another tonality to help us create a more interesting line. Lots of jazz players apply this kind of modal thinking to their playing.

In bar two we have another implied harmony idea borrowed from jazz. In a jazz blues, the IV chord (Eb) is often followed by a diminished 7 chord a half step above before returning to the I chord (Bb). The lick here hints that the underlying chord could be Edim7 (E G Bb Db), a half step above Eb7.

In bar four there is more implied harmony as the melodic line suggests the sound of G7.

Example 1n

For the turnaround section, we return to F Mixolydian to spell out the sound of the F7 chord, then go to some Bb Minor Pentatonic vocabulary to end with a bluesy phrase.

Example 1o

Example 1p uses a simple repeating motif on the second and third strings. Notice that in bars 2-4 the idea is delayed by an 1/8th note each time, so that it sounds less predictable.

Example 1p

If Example 1p was the question, this lick is the answer. It takes the theme and embellishes it on the first string.

Example 1q

Repetition is a key idea in the blues and is still one of the simplest yet most effective strategies to create a vocal-like performance that makes the guitar sing. This line is all about the articulation, so check out the audio carefully.

In bar four I play one of my favorite licks which uses a hybrid scale. Most of the notes come from the Bb Mixolydian scale (Bb C D Eb F G Ab), so we're viewing the I chord as if it's a V chord. Then, I like to throw in a chromatic note from outside the key to create a brief tension that is quickly resolved. Look out for it in the second group of triplets. For the last few notes of the phrase, the line transitions into the Bb Blues scale to bring things back home.

Example 1r

To close out this chapter, here's a two-chorus solo for you to try. Listen out for the themes I introduce here and how they are developed. Check out the audio first and have a couple of listens all the way through before attempting the solo.

Example 1s – Solo

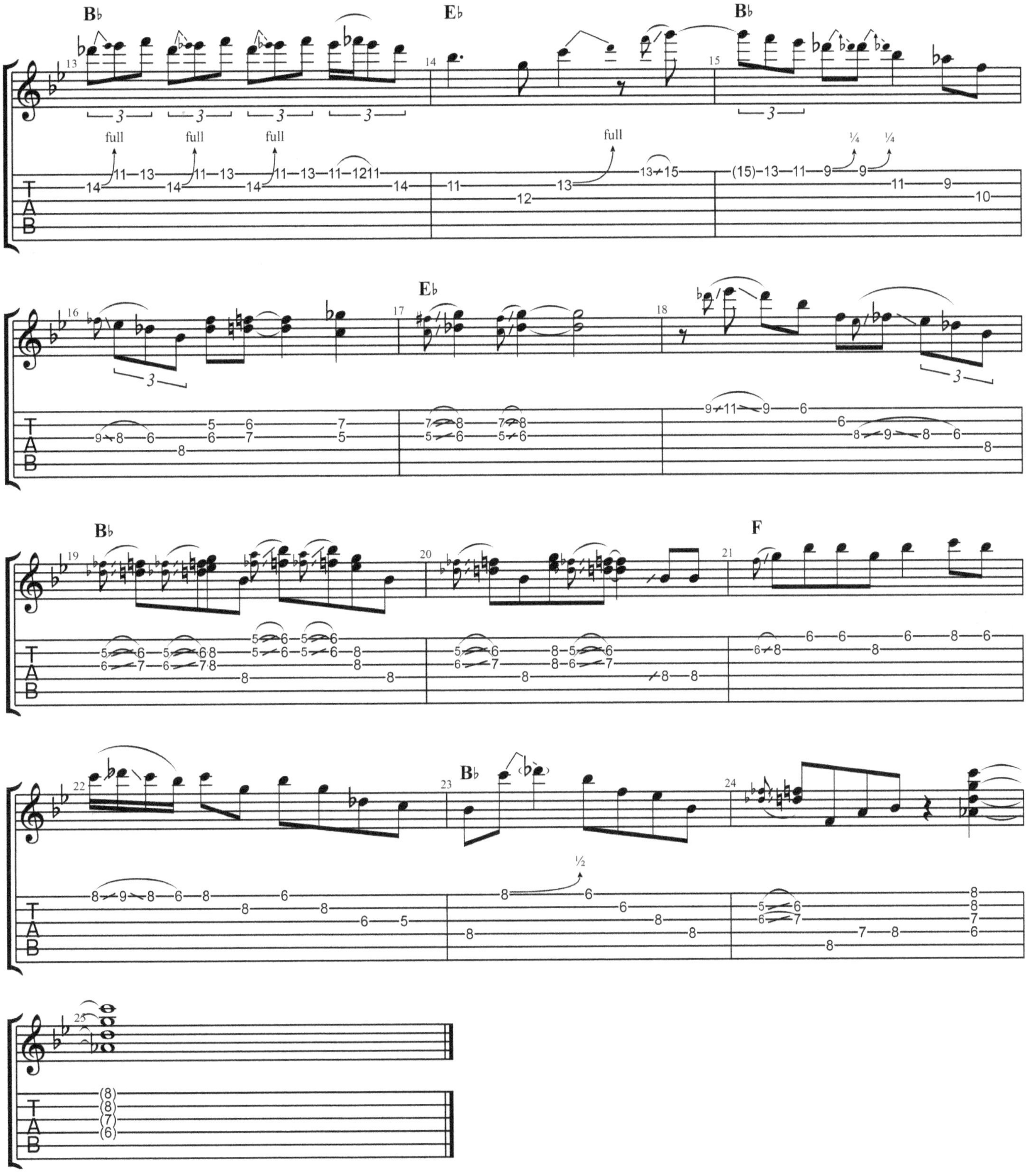
B♭
E♭
B♭
full
full
full
full
¼
¼
E♭
B♭
F
B♭
½

Chapter Two – Funky Blues

The musical genre of funk, which emerged during the mid-60s, is a melting pot of styles influenced by blues, gospel, soul and jazz. But what goes around, comes around, and the syncopated rhythms that developed around funk have always found their way back into the blues. In this chapter, we'll look at a funky, New Orleans-style blues and see how modern blues vocabulary can work over a tune with a very different feel to that of the previous chapter.

Every song we play over will give us clues about how to apply our vocabulary in that situation. First of all, the style and the vibe of the song will suggest that we play different things. The tempo will also dictate how and what we play. And then the key signature will also open up different ideas – ways we can use our licks in different zones of the neck; how we might access parts of the fretboard that only open up when playing in a particular key, etc.

I often talk about having a *roadmap* for a tune. All these things – tempo, key, vibe – are the "road markers" we need to read and respond to when improvising. Playing the blues is all about responding to the music and connecting with the ideas that the tune is crying out for.

We tend to think of improvisation as an in-the-moment, entirely unplanned, spontaneous thing, but really that's only half the story. In order to improvise we draw upon a library of ideas – all the things we've learned over the years.

What I've set out to do here is to give you some vocabulary for "planned improvisation" in a range of settings that crop up time and again in the blues. Learning these phrases and adapting them, so that they sound like you, is your preparation for improvisation. The more you know, and the more you connect with the vibe of a tune, the more you'll be able to express the music that you hear in your head.

Applying some more jazz influence to the blues

When I was in my teens, I had an older friend who was a jazz guitarist. He would often listen to me play and told me that I needed to get some new ideas into my repertoire of licks. One day he got me to play rhythm for him while he took a solo and I made a little half step approach as I changed to the IV chord. He stopped me and said, "What did you just do?"

"You mean this?" I asked.

"Yeah," he said, "do that when you're soloing."

It was a lightbulb moment for me. I realized that I could instantly sound more interesting by using this simple idea, borrowed from jazz, of playing approach notes to "target" chord tones. We discussed this briefly in the previous chapter. The idea is to pick a note to aim for, then use passing notes to get there. A passing note can either be a scale tone or a chromatic tone (from outside the key). Scale tone passing notes sound *inside* the harmony while chromatic passing notes sound *outside*.

A key to this technique is to hit chord or scale tones on the down beats of the bar and chromatic notes on the up beats. You can play outside as much as you want, as long as you hit an "inside" note on the beat and it'll sound great. I'll use this idea in the examples that follow, so look out for it.

(NB: In this tune, I'm frequently thinking of each chord in the tune as a static V chord, so the examples here are notated with no key signature. This way it's easier to see what's going on).

As before, you can connect every three examples together to form a complete chorus of the blues, and Example 2a is an opening statement for the solo.

An idea used constantly in the blues is to emphasize the major third of the dominant chord (a B note in the case of G7) and the easiest way to do this is to approach it from the minor 3rd (Bb), a half step below. You can hear this idea in bars 3-4.

In bars 2-3 I'm using the notes of the G Mixolydian scale (G A B C D E F), viewing the G7 as a V chord rather than the tonic.

Bar four contains a lick I like to use where I emphasize the 6th and 9th intervals of the dominant chord (E and A respectively over G7). Both notes are in the G Mixolydian scale.

Example 2a

The next lick features some jazz-influenced chromatic approach notes. In bar one, the Eb note on the second string is targeting the E note on the open first string, the 3rd of C7 (C E G Bb). I allow those two notes to ring into each other to create a little dissonance. Bar two uses one chromatic passing note on the second string and you should recognize this country-inspired lick.

The rest of the lick is arranged in double-stops in either thirds or sixths, and the phrase includes several chromatic approaches from a half step below.

Example 2b

The next example is the turnaround section of the tune. In the pickup bar and bar one I play a phrase with two chromatic passing notes. The phrase is based around D Mixolydian (D E F# G A B C) and the passing notes on the second and third strings help to connect the scale tones for a more fluid line.

In bar one, the chromatic run down on the third string targets the b7 (C) of the D7 chord. This motif is then adapted to fit over the C7 chord in bar two, where the run down in the first half of the bar also hits the b7.

Bars 3-4 conclude the idea with a bluesy lick using G Mixolydian.

Example 2c

This lick begins with a double chromatic approach (i.e. playing two approach notes to target a note from above or below) which leads into an Em7 arpeggio lick.

This lick also features an *enclosure* idea in the first half of bar three, borrowed from jazz, similar to the one we looked at in Chapter One. Here, the idea is to pick a target note (the G note on the first string, 3rd fret, that falls on beat 2), then play a chromatic note a half step below it (F#, fret 2) and a scale tone above it (A, fret 5).

There are more half step sliding chromatic notes in bars 3-4.

Example 2d

To create vocal-like phrases that evoke an emotional response in your audience, bending notes and playing phrases that cross the bar line are two very powerful tools. The next lick anticipates beat 1 of bar one by beginning on the "3&" of the pickup bar with a bend. A vocal effect is achieved by playing another bend immediately after it.

After the phrase in bar one, I leave some breathing space before beginning the next idea in bar two, and this phrase spills over into bar three. After an 1/8th note rest, the final phrase also bridges bars 3-4.

Example 2e

To bring some variety into the sound, for the opening of the next lick I briefly switch to the D Blues scale (D F G Ab A C) in the pickup bar, then to the D Minor scale (D E F G A Bb C) in bar one, with one added chromatic passing note.

In bar two I'm using the C Mixolydian scale (C D E F G A Bb) to play a phrase that carries over into bar three. This lick is all about the articulation, so have a careful listen to the audio to hear how I slide between notes and also hang onto the blues curl bend in bar two for a more vocal sound.

Example 2f

The next idea uses a variety of techniques to create a lick with plenty of interest. Let's break it down.

First, blues curls (notated as quarter note bends) are used throughout bars 1-2, and this series of bends is what gives the phrase its vocal-like articulation.

The notes for this lick come from the G Blues scale (G Bb C Db D F) but the scale isn't used in the conventional sense to play bluesy clichés. Instead, I'm targeting the scale's Db note, which is the b5 interval over the underlying G7 chord, and this gives the lick its outside-inside sound, especially at the end of bar two going into bar three.

The second idea here is the fast, repeating rhythmic motif that spans the end of bar three into bar four. This idea contains string skipping and I tend to play this kind of idea using hybrid picking, though it is possible to flat pick it. (In the next chapter I'll explain the technique I use for hybrid picking).

To play this triplet lick, which begins on beat 4 of bar three, I suggest fretting the top two strings at the 8th fret with the first finger, and the third string, 9th fret, with the second finger. Keep these fingers in place throughout the lick and play the adjacent notes with the fourth or third finger. Slow things right down to begin with to get your picking/fretting hand movements in place before bringing it up to tempo.

Example 2g

In bar one of the next example, a short sliding phrase in thirds spells out the major 3rd (E) and 5th (G) of C7. In bar two I modify this idea to flatten the 3rd to Eb and spell C minor for contrast.

In bars 3-4, over the G7 chord, I play a melodic motif. In bar three the full idea is expressed, then bar four has a shortened version. Throughout, an E note is emphasized, with is the 13th interval and implies the sound of G13.

Example 2h

The trickiest part of the next line is the fast run over the C7 chord in bar two, where triplets are grouped in sixes. Whereas previously we've used the C Mixolydian scale for this chord, here we're switching to the C Natural Minor (C D Eb F G Ab Bb) scale. However, we're also borrowing the b5 (Gb) note from the C Blues scale to complete the picture.

If you're just playing with a bassist who's holding down the C root note at this point, this will just sound like an idea that blurs the major/minor tonality of the blues. If you're playing with rhythm guitar or keys, and they are playing a C7 chord here, the effect is quite different.

Over C7, the C Natural Minor scale includes the root, 5th and b7 of the chord. The scale also has an Eb note, which is a potential clash with the major 3rd (E) of C7, but in a lick like this, Eb is just a brief passing note that is quickly resolved. The remaining scale tones all represent extended or altered notes over C7. The D, F, Ab and the Gb note we borrowed are, in order, the 9th, 11th, #5 and #11 of C7. So, superimposing a C minor scale over C7 is a quick hack to instantly achieve a richer, more complex harmony.

Example 2i

The next idea aims to keep things interesting with rhythmic variation. In the pickup bar, on beat "3&" a 1/16th note run begins the lick. In bar one, as the 1/16th note line continues, string skips are introduced and the D note on the fourth string 12th fret acts briefly as a pedal tone. On beat 3 of bar one, slower bends are introduced to break up the predictable rhythm.

In bar two, another 1/16th note phrase begins, with 1/32nd note articulations, and this carries over to the beginning of bar three. In the latter half of bar three a quick ascending run transitions into the more complex idea of bar four.

Bar four is a G Blues scale lick that, after the first odd-note grouping of seven, becomes a 1/16th note triplet line. To learn it, I suggest breaking it down into four separate units, as indicated in the notation, then joining them back together.

Overall, I hope you can see that this lick is all about applying different rhythms to the phrases. It keeps the listener engaged and stops things from getting boring.

Example 2j

Here's another lick driven by syncopation and rhythmic variety.

Bars 1-2 rely on 1/16th note triplets with the notes coming from the G Minor Pentatonic and G Blues scales. To play this rhythmic motif, hold down the top part of a simple G minor chord shape at the 15th fret. The first finger should remain in place, holding down the second and third strings at the 15th fret, while the third finger frets the notes at the 17th fret on the third and fourth strings.

I tend to hybrid pick a lick like this, using a combination of pick and fingers, but it's possible to economy pick it by pushing the pick downward through the strings then raking it back up.

In bar three, the rhythmic feel changes to rocky straight 1/16ths but this motif is converted to 1/16th note triplets again in bar four. Take some time to work out your fingerings with this one, as it can be difficult to keep things sounding clear, especially when using overdrive.

Example 2k

In this turnaround example, the line begins with a simple descending idea in 6ths played on non-adjacent strings. This part of the line ends on the "2a" of bar two, and a new idea begins on beat 3. This is a pedal tone lick that keeps the Bb note on the third string, 15th fret, going throughout. To create some rhythmic surprise, I also play it with a staccato feel to punch out the notes.

Example 2l

Now for another line that moves between major and minor tonalities. The lick freely alternates the major 3rd and b3 of the underlying chord and also adds in the b5 interval from the blues scale.

Example 2m

Next up is a line that begins with a complete contrast to the kind of melodic ideas we've used so far. Over the G7 chord in the pickup bar I decided to focus on the minor tonality of the blues, but this time used the G Melodic Minor scale (G A Bb C D E Gb) – although I still added in the b5 note (Db) from the G Blues scale!

The first nine notes of the pickup bar all come from this augmented G Melodic Minor scale. The last six-note grouping is the straight G Natural Minor scale. Though both are well-used scales, the intervallic arrangement of this lick adds to the feeling that it sounds "outside".

In bars 1-2, over the C7 chord, I switch to the C Mixolydian scale for a straighter bluesy lick, and this idea flows into the G Blues scale lick that closes out bars 3-4. Notice the mix of triplet and straight 1/16th notes to keep the rhythmic variety interesting.

Example 2n

For the turnaround that completes this set of three examples, the minor 3rd is played again over the major 3rd of the D7 chord in bar one. In bar two, an A note is emphasized over the C7 chord, which implies a C13 sound, and a straight G Mixolydian lick completes the blues chorus in bars 3-4. When playing the bends, make sure you squeeze out of them every ounce of expression and feeling you can.

Example 2o

To conclude this chapter, here's a complete two-chorus solo that uses many of the ideas we've discussed. Break it into sections to learn it, then try it over the included backing track.

Example 2p – Solo

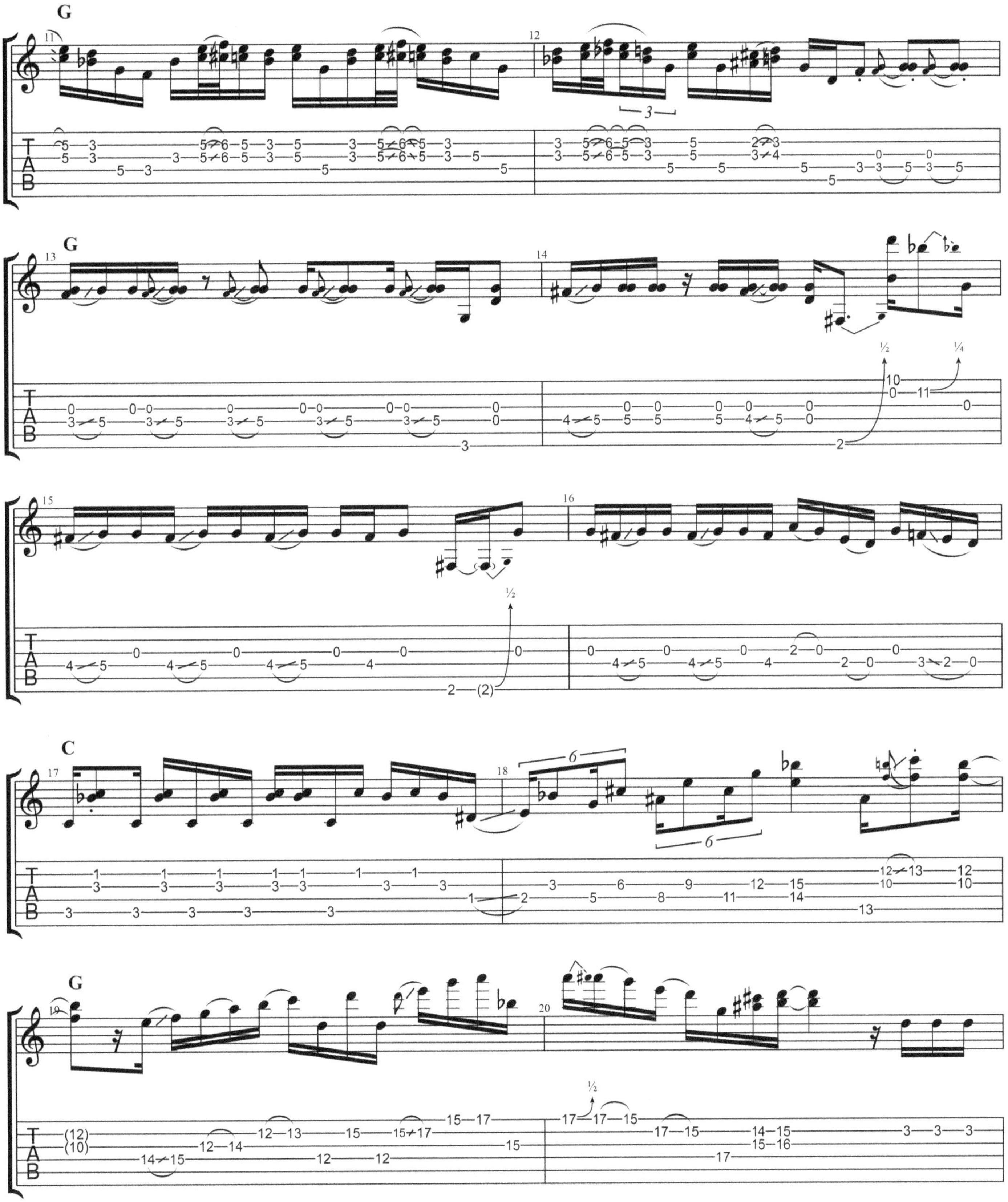
G
G
C
G

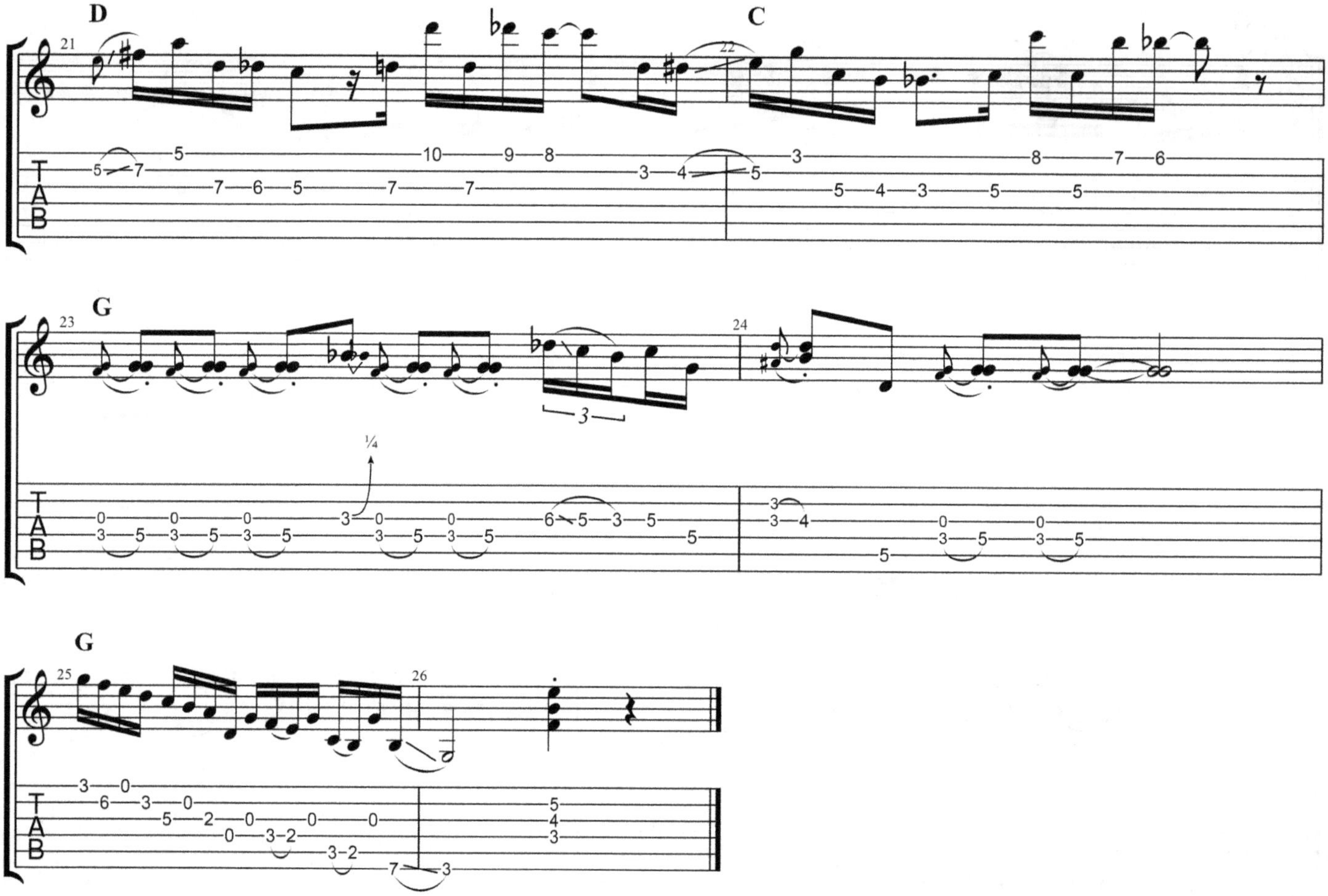
D
C
G
G

Chapter Three – Jump Blues

Jump blues is a style that dates back to the 1940s and was the precursor to RnB and Rock 'n' Roll. It originated in the big bands of artists like Cab Calloway and Lionel Hampton, and is always played up tempo with a distinct jazz influence infused into the blues. Musicians like saxophonist Louis Jordan and others took the style outside of the big band context and pioneered its use in smaller combos, and this helped lay the foundations of RnB. Jump blues became the bridge between the old and the new.

Musical trends come and go, but Jump blues was an important part of the *swing revival* of the 1990s and has an ongoing place as part of the popularity of Rockabilly and blues music around the world. In this chapter we're going to look some of the language I've developed around this style – which more than any other type of blues makes me want to combine country and jazz ideas that fit with the celebratory, up-beat nature of the music.

Jump blues has a "double-time" feel and the drummer will often play a fast "freight train" style rhythm on the snare. For this reason, the 12-bar blues sequence has been notated as a 24-bar structure in the examples that follow. When the tempo is this fast, and there are a lot of notes, it's significantly easier to read it this way.

To play this style of blues efficiently, personally I prefer to use hybrid picking technique. So, before we look at the licks, let me briefly explain my approach.

Hybrid Picking Technique

For years I played with the pick gripped between my thumb and first finger, and the rest of my fingers anchored to the body of the guitar for stability. That was until someone gave me a tape that had Danny Gatton on one side and Roy Lanham on the other. Danny's modern country playing became very influential and important to my development, and Roy's jazz-influenced country was also amazing and inspiring.

When I listened to Danny's mind-boggling licks, I realized that they depended on a different picking technique. It just wasn't possible to flatpick most of them, and even if I could, they still didn't sound as good. Danny's licks had a very clean sound to them, with great note separation. One of the first things I tried to learn was his version of Ray Charles' *What'd I Say*, which he plays at warp speed. It sounded terrible flatpicked. Of course, Danny was using hybrid picking, so that's when I switched to hybrid and began to develop playing with that technique.

Hybrid picking just means to use the pick and fingers of the picking hand in combination. As with most technique-driven concepts, everyone hybrid picks slightly differently, in a way that feels comfortable to them. There's no single "right way" to do it, only what works for you and sounds good. I'll explain how I approach it – and you can try my way – but you'll want to experiment and find your own take on it. Either way, it's worth exploring this technique because it allows you to play licks that can't be achieved any other way.

Hybrid triplets

First, I grip the pick with my thumb and first finger and use my second and third fingers for plucking strings. The pinkie finger is rarely, if ever, used. When I started to teach myself this style, I quickly noticed that my second finger naturally began to replace pick upstrokes.

I analysed what I was doing, and what felt natural to me, and discovered that I played a lot of licks that use a *pick-pick-finger* pattern. By this, I mean playing two pick strokes on adjacent strings, followed by a pluck with the second finger.

The idea is to play two *downward* pick strokes by pushing through adjacent strings with one motion, then pluck *upward* with the second finger. This lends itself to playing triplet patterns, like country banjo rolls. Try it now. Palm mute the strings with the picking hand so that the notes don't sustain, then slowly pick this triplet pattern.

Exercise 1

If you've never hybrid picked before, this may feel a little awkward to begin with, but stick with it. The above exercise is the kind of thing you can practice with your guitar unplugged, sitting in front of the TV, because it's just about training the mechanical movement of your pick/fingers into muscle memory. I used to spend hours doing this until the movement became second nature.

When you're confident with the above exercise, try moving between string sets to play these A major triads.

Exercise 2

The *pick-pick finger* approach is fundamental to my personal hybrid picking style, and I do play a lot of triplet figures, as you'll see in the licks that follow. There are other ways to approach it, of course, and you may find you're comfortable using a different technique. There are actually very few guidebooks that explain how to do it, apart from Levi Clay's excellent *Hybrid Picking Guitar Technique*, which covers the topic in great detail.

Hybrid double-stops

I use hybrid picking slightly differently (especially in a Jump blues context) when playing double-stop licks. Here, I use the combination of a single downward pick stroke and an upward finger pluck. I also pluck upward using the second and third fingers together for added power, to create more of a snap and achieve a more aggressive tone. Here's a double-stop exercise for you to test this out.

Exercise 3

Hybrid 6ths

It also helps to have hybrid picking technique under your fingers if you want to play passages in 6ths, country style. Try this simple line, which requires you to pick downward and pluck upward simultaneously with a pinching motion. After a bit of practice, you'll find it much easier to execute 6th lines hybrid, rather than adjusting the fretting hand position to try and mute the string in between the fretted notes.

Exercise 4

Once you begin to get into this style of picking, you may find that you want to hybrid pick much more than just the licks that demand it. I found that I began to play hybrid a lot of the time, and I liked being able to jump between wider intervals and play lines with a smoother, cleaner technique with good note separation. Nowadays, I can't play as fast as I used to using standard flatpicking technique, but I can pick way faster than I used to using hybrid!

I also found that, after a while, even if I was just using the pick, I kept my hand floating rather than anchored to the body of the guitar. Keeping the picking hand in the floating position means it's very easy to switch between hybrid and flatpicking as needed.

I will also sometimes put the pick away and play purely fingerstyle for a specific effect. That could be to play softer, but also to play harder and really snap the strings for a more cutting tone.

Many of the licks here can be played with standard flat picking technique, but where you see passages of triplets across strings, 6ths, or wider interval jumps, I'll be hybrid picking, so do give it a go.

This jump blues is in the key of E Major and as in previous chapters, every three examples can be combined to form a full-chorus solo.

This opening lick uses sparse phrasing and allows plenty of space to establish the groove. Although we are in E Major, I'm treating the E as a V chord and using the E Mixolydian scale (E F# G# A B C# D) to create the melodic line. Notice that I'm also making use of open strings where possible. Try hybrid picking this line to achieve the same tone as the audio recording.

Example 3a

In the next example, I reuse the simple phrase that began the previous example but adapt it for the A chord. I'm using the idea of "whatever idea you play first, that's your theme", discussed back in Chapter One. This is a great way of being spontaneous with improvisation, but also focused, as we have to apply some thought to keep the theme going and be creative with it.

At this stage of the solo, where ideas are developing, notice that I'm still leaving quite a lot of space.

Example 3b

For the turnaround section of the tune, I keep the motif going on the top two strings and use open strings where possible. The same notes create different intervals when played over different chords and in bar one, the D note on the second string that is emphasized here is the #9 interval over B7.

If you can, use a combination of pick and fingers to play this entire line, as the notes will ring into each other in a pleasing way. This works especially well for the lick that begins on beat 4 of bar five. It's an E Mixolydian line that uses hammer-ons and open strings, and ends by anticipating the B7 chord ahead of bar eight.

Example 3c

The theme continues in the next example, with many of the ideas played on the top two strings around 2nd position. The most difficult part of this lick is the country-inspired descending run in bars 5-8, that moves outside of the theme.

In bars 5-6 I'm using the E Blues scale (E G A Bb B D) for a minor sound over the harmony but by bars 7-8 this has transitioned back into E Mixolydian. Hybrid pick this to achieve the recorded sound and articulation and let those open strings ring out against the fretted notes. Slow things down and work out your fingerings before attempting it at full tempo.

Example 3d

In this line, the A7 harmony is introduced with a simple root and 5th chord. In bar two, I'm playing the E Blues scale over the A chord. In bar three, a double-stop outlines the A7 chord again, this time using the 3rd and 5th. As the line continues, it transitions into E Mixolydian in bar five as the progression returns to the E7 chord. For the rest of the lick you'll hear that I alternate between highlighting the major and minor 3rd of E7, as in bar seven.

Example 3e

Here's an idea that begins by playing a fast A major triad that slides up a whole step to a B major triad over the B7 chord. The chord changes have been on E7 previously, so this is a little surprise to the ears.

The great thing about the blues is that, if you want, you can solo over the whole progression with just one scale and in bar three I use the E Blues scale again to create the melody. To end this lick, bars 6-7 use a popular idea, which is to approach the 3rd and 5th of the E7 chord chromatically from above. Bar six is the approach and we hit the chord tones on beat 1 of bar seven.

Example 3f

Since we're playing in the key of E Major, it makes sense to utilize the open strings wherever possible, so here is a common doubling-up lick, where the open high E string is paired with a sliding E note on the second string. You'll have heard this kind of lick before, but make sure you mute the lower strings to get the phrase sounding cleanly. In bars 3-4 and 7-8, aim to use hybrid picking to get the pull-off phrase sounding smooth.

Example 3g

In contrast to the previous example, here's a more challenging lick for you to try, which is less scalic and more intervallic.

In bars 1-3 the lick is an A Mixolydian scale sequence that incorporates several open strings and morphs into the A Blues scale for the last few notes of bar three.

In the latter half of bar five a pedal tone idea begins that carries through the next two bars. In bars 6-7 you can see that the intervals get wider as the line progresses. The B note on the fourth string 9th fret is the pedal tone that continues throughout, and the notes that bounce off it comes from the E Mixolydian scale.

Example 3h

Example 3i begins with a chromatic descending lick to spell out the B7 chord, and includes both the major and minor 3rd of the chord. In bar three I begin a rhythmic idea that occurred to me in the moment, which I continue to the end of the lick. Motifs can be created from note choices but also from rhythmic choices. If you ever feel short of ideas to play, choose rhythm and groove above notes. Play something simple and groove the crap out of it!

In bar three, the idea begins on the root of the A chord and plays an A Major triad. At the end of bar four, instead of playing the expected G note (the b7 of A7), G# is used (the 3rd of E7) to anticipate the E chord.

Example 3i

Next up is a rhythmically challenging lick for you. Bars 1-4 make use of some dotted 1/4 notes to create a staccato effect, which really helps to punch those notes out. This section begins with a country flavor but becomes more intervallic in bars 3-4.

In bar three, the idea I had was to pick an E Mixolydian scale tone (I opted for C#, the 6th of the underlying E7 chord) and use it as a pedal tone. The notes that bounce off it are scale tones where the intervals become wider (starting with a 4th, 5th, then 6th).

Bar five contains a rhythmically similar idea to bar one, and bar six is a double-stop lick. This is ideally played using hybrid picking. It's possible to play it without but do give it a try if you can.

For rhythmic variety, an E Major triad is played with a fast triplet in bar seven, leading into the final descending run which echoes the rhythmic approach of bars one and five.

Example 3j

Next up is an idea that uses a typical box position pentatonic shape to create a classic lick. In bars 1-4 I'm using the A Major Pentatonic scale (A B C# E F#) and this transitions into E Mixolydian for bars 5-8 (the last note of bar four anticipates the change).

Be sure to execute the sliding double-stops of bar five cleanly and the unexpected 4th intervals that follow in bar six.

Example 3k

For the turnaround section of this blues sequence, we start with octave bends in bar one. This type of idea can sound messy when using overdrive if it's not executed cleanly. We want the two notes to bleed into one another to create a unison A note, as that's the point of the lick, but if you're hearing unwanted general string noise then use a little picking hand palm muting to keep things under control.

To keep things interesting on the return to the E chord in this lick I played some wider intervals using hybrid picking in bars 5-6. In bar six, beginning on beat 4 with a B note, the line ascends the E Mixolydian scale in sequence. The rest of the line weaves around the chord tones adding in some chromatic passing notes.

Example 3l

Example 3m uses a fast, hybrid picked motif throughout with varied rhythms, combining 1/4 notes and 1/8th notes. I recommend holding down the E Major triad shape on which this lick is based throughout. Hold down the 14th fret on the D string with the third finger. Your second and first fingers will naturally fall onto the third string 13th fret, and second string 12th fret, respectively.

For bars 1-2 keep the third finger fixed in place and slide into the double-stops with the first and second fingers. In bars 3-4 you can keep the third finger where it is but roll and flatten on the fretboard to play the 14th fret double-stop on the second/third strings. Play the 12th fret double-stop at the beginning of bar four with the first finger.

That covers the technique, it just gets faster toward the end!

Example 3m

The next lick is more challenging and hybrid picking is the best approach to play this one smoothly at the required tempo. It looks intimidating on paper with its different rhythmic groupings of notes, but like the previous lick, for bars 1-2 you can hold down the same shape throughout.

This time, hold down an E minor chord shape in 12th position. Your third finger will hold down the 14th fret on the fourth string, while your first finger barres the top three strings at the 12th. Don't move your hand from this position and use your fourth finger to play all the notes on the top three strings that bounce off that E pedal tone.

When coming out of the lick midway through bar three, watch out for the timing of the line in bars 3-4. Check out the audio to get the exact timing. In bars 5-8 the line begins to descend, making use of a quick E9 chord punctuation and 6th intervals.

Example 3n

Here's another lick that makes use of 6ths, this time in the lower register to turn around the tune. You'll need to hybrid pick this one, or put away your pick and use your fingers to pluck the notes.

Example 3o

To kick off the next group of three examples, here's an opening line that uses a simple but effective chordal idea and is the kind of thing that can work really well to thicken the sound if you're playing in a trio with bass and drums. The main chord in use looks like a C# minor shape, but over the E bass note creates an E6 sound. A riff is created by moving this shape a half step below and back again.

The descending run in bars 7-8 is based around the E Blues scale. I included open strings where possible and also added in a couple of chromatic passing notes.

Example 3p

In a similar vein to the previous example, over the A7 chord section here's a line that also utilizes open strings and features a passing note descending run to target the E7 chord in bar five.

The lick in bar six is the same four notes repeated up an octave each time, but we break away from that idea on beat 2 of bar seven. The slides are an important part of this lick, so listen to the audio to nail the articulation.

Example 3q

To complete the 12-bar chorus, here's an idea for the turnaround section that uses the tools of *repetition* and *rhythmic displacement*. From bar three, the same descending phrase is repeated through to the end of bar seven.

First of all, repeating an idea like this is a key part of blues phrasing and we use it when we want to make a strong musical statement. Second, the phrase is made up of six 1/8th notes and is repeated without a rest.

The effect of this is to constantly *shift* the phrase so that it begins on different beats of the bar. In bar three, the lick begins on beat 3, which means that in bar four it falls on beat 2, and in bar five on beat 1, etc.

See if you can invent your own similar phrase that will automatically shift position across multiple bars. Practice this idea to the backing track.

Example 3r

Here is another repetition idea, this time using a single note, as the root of the E7 chord is emphasized. As guitar players, we often like to play lots of notes – that's just our nature – but the truth is, so much can be done with just one or two notes, especially in the blues where feeling is valued above virtuosity. Check it out!

Example 3s

The theme of the previous lick continues here. Over the A7 chord, the root and b7 are emphasized. As the chords change to E7, this idea is kept going with a slight modification, as the A note slides into a B. The B and G notes together imply an E Minor rather than E Major tonality.

Example 3t

The line that begins in bar three and spans all the way into bar six is the most difficult part of this next idea and calls for some rapid finger slides.

It begins with a very fast half step slide on the second string. At the end of bar three, slide from 10th to 12th fret with the third finger. Play the first string 10th fret with the first finger, and the 12th with the third finger, then slide the third finger quickly up to the 15th fret. Allow the first finger to come behind it to fret the first string 12th fret and you'll be in position for the rest of the lick. Make sure you wring every ounce of emotion out of the full step bends in bars six and seven.

Example 3u

Now it's time to attempt a full two-chorus solo. It contains many of the phrasing ideas we've looked at in this chapter, but the first twelve bars present a few rhythmic curveballs for you to check out.

I suggest isolating the lick in bars 3-4 to begin with and nailing the phrasing there. Similar to the polyrhythmic lick you learnt in Example 3n, you can play this lick by holding down a partial E minor barre chord shape in 12th position and playing the moving notes with the fourth finger.

In terms of rhythm, the first three notes are 1/16th note triplets and are followed by two straight 1/8th notes. Then there are two straight 1/16th notes, after which the phrase loops around. Listen to the audio a few times then slow things right down and work on the rhythmic timing until you can keep looping the phrase around without making a mistake. Only then should you work on speeding it up.

Also look out for the change in rhythm in bar nine, where we switch to using all 1/8th note triplets.

During the first twelve bars I used hybrid picking exclusively. It's not impossible to play this flat picked, but if you're developing hybrid style, use this as an exercise to practice your coordination.

Example 3v – Solo

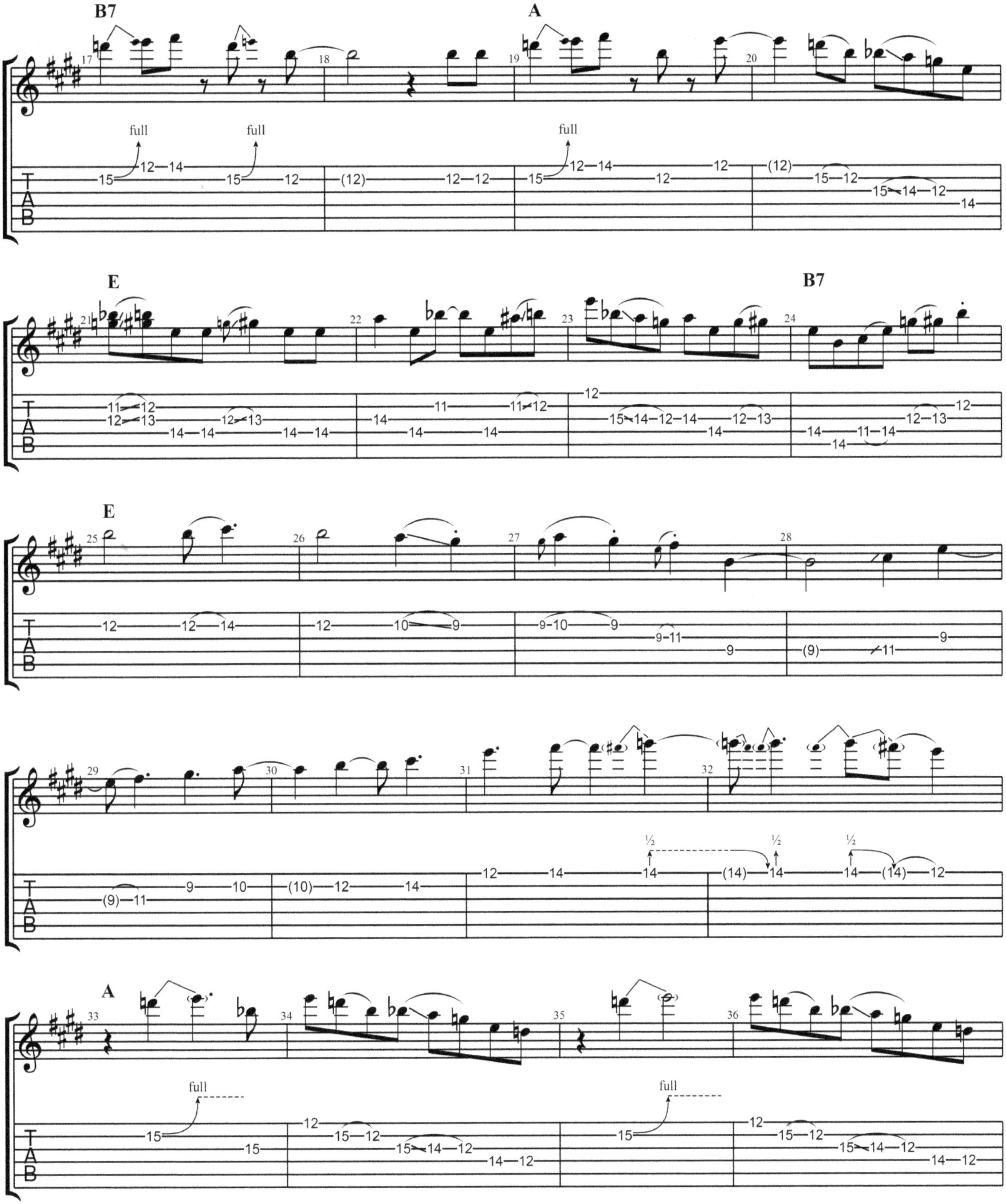
B7
A
full
E
B7
E
½
A
full

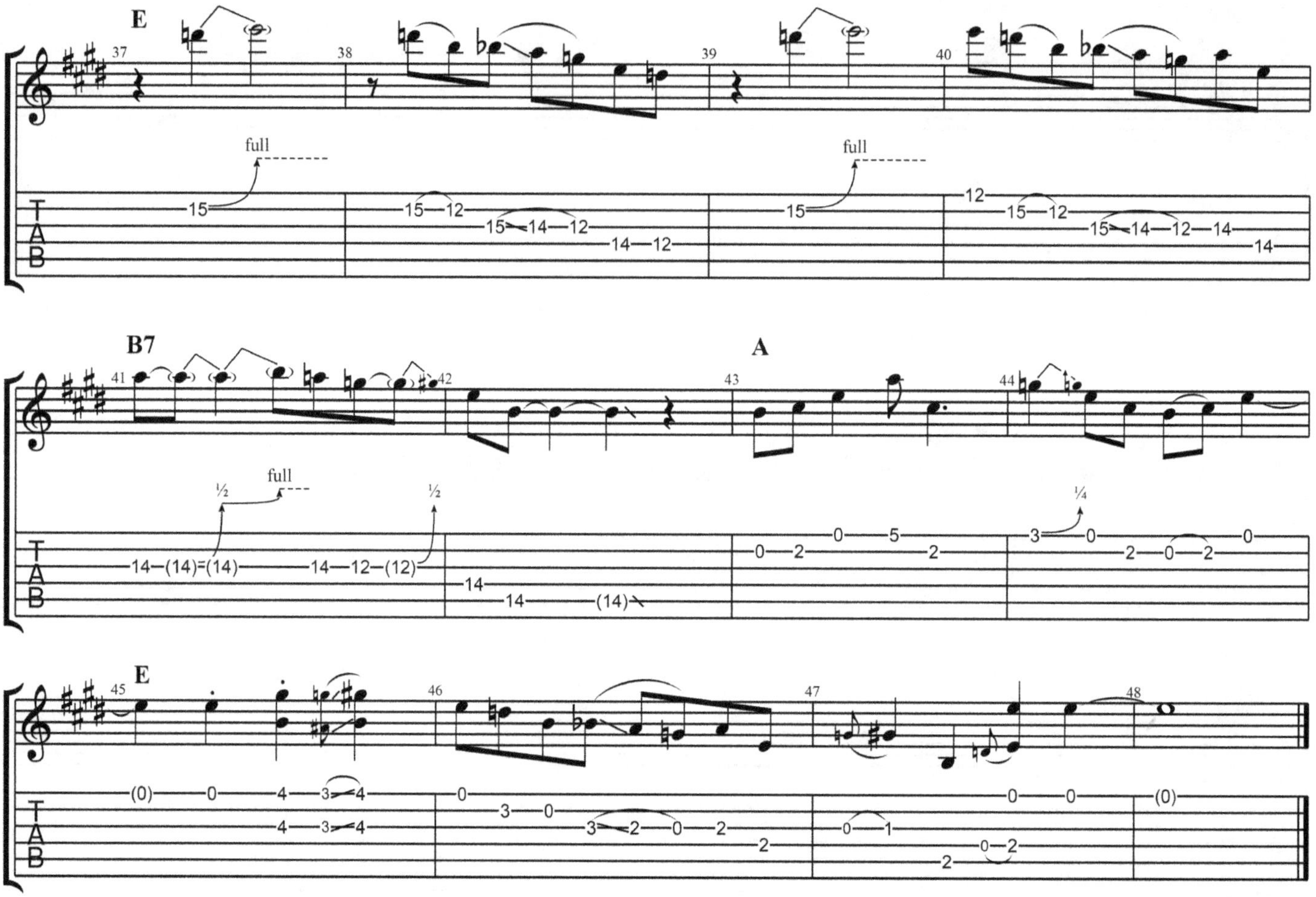
E
full
full
B7
½
full
½
A
¼
E
TAB

Chapter Four – Slow Blues Ballad

The great thing about the blues is that it can take many forms. In the previous chapter we looked at the most up-tempo form of this music and now we will look at one of its moodiest, soulful and most introspective expressions – the slow blues ballad.

Strictly speaking, the term "ballad" just refers to a narrative folk song. Going back to the roots of the blues, ballads were a way of cataloging events. They told tales of murders, unfaithfulness and other heartaches, or simply recalled the highlights of someone's life. But over the years the term ballad has come to mean a slow-tempo blues that is a showcase for emotionally charged, expressive playing. Go back to the 1966 recording of *Red House* by Jimi Hendrix, for example, and you'll get the picture. It's an example of storytelling and emotive playing. There have been hundreds of great examples since.

In this chapter, the slow blues is played in 12/8 time signature. You'll hear that the backing is quite sparse and laid back and this opens up a lot of space for the soloist to use. Tracks like this can be very exposing when you are the main melodic instrument, so it's good to have a collection of solid ideas to fall back on, and some good blues vocabulary appropriate to this kind of track.

In this chapter, you'll need to focus especially hard on achieving the right feel and capturing the articulation of each line. Much more important than the notes being played is the emotion you invest in each line. If the blues is about one thing, it's about attitude and playing with confidence and conviction.

This track is in the key of B Major. As usual, blurring the major/minor tonality of the blues, we'll draw on both B Major and B Minor ideas.

Example 4a is a typical "opening statement". It's important to start strong and play a decisive opening phrase and the opening lick in the pickup bar and bar one is simple and all about the attitude with which it's played. The notes come from the B Blues scale (B D E F F# A).

In bar two, over the E7 chord, I play another B Blues scale lick, but then switch to E Mixolydian (E F# G# A B C# D) for a phrase that spans the end of bar two and bar three.

Notice how the lick moves between short punchy phrases and faster flurries of notes.

The lick ends with a stripped back voicing of B9.

Example 4a

Stevie Ray Vaughn and Albert King thrived in this kind of blues territory and some of the triplet phrases in this next idea are a nod to those two great players.

In bar one, the mix of half and quarter note bends are used to give a vocal-like articulation to the phrase. In bars 2-3, and again in bar four, a similar idea is used with slides and a quarter note blues curl adding to the expression.

(NB: It is notoriously difficult to notate these playing nuances in a meaningful way, so listen to the audio for every example to capture the feel and timing).

Example 4b

Even when the backing you're playing over is sparse, don't be afraid to still leave space. It's very tempting to think, "There's not much happening so I'll fill out the sound with more notes." There are times when it's appropriate to do this for an effect but most of the time, less is more.

The next example, which is the turnaround section of this blues, can be broken down into a series of short phrases with rests between each one. It's really important to "breath" between phrases. If you can, sing along quietly with your playing, so that you are forced to take an *actual* breath – or if that's too embarrassing, vocalize in your head. Either way, try to avoid moving from one idea to the next without pausing. Instead, discipline yourself to play a complete phrase then take a breath before starting the next one.

You might notice the Hendrix-style double-stops combined with a hammer-on in bars 3-4 of this lick.

Example 4c

As we start on a second chorus of the blues, here's another example where I'm working really hard to achieve vocal phrasing and infuse every note with as much emotion as possible. First of all, have a listen to the audio. How can you set about achieving a similar sound? Here are two keys for you:

- Tone – first, you can achieve an incredible amount of variation in tone simply by moving your picking hand slightly forward or backward. Pick nearer the neck and you'll get a warmer, more glassy tone. Pick nearer the bridge and you'll get a more biting tone. In fact, you don't have to move far in either direction to alter the tone; subtle movements can add a lot of contrast.

- Dynamics – in this lick I pick some phrases aggressively for a cutting, attention-grabbing tone but then pull right back and pick some phrases softly. This also affects the tone, but its main purpose is to create the effect of a conversation. It's another form of the question and answer of the blues, where a loud statement is answered by a quiet one, and it sounds like two complementary parts are being played.

Example 4d

In the next example there is a balance between longer held notes and fast runs composed with 1/16th or 1/32nd notes.

To learn the lick, begin by isolating the phrase in bar one. I vary the dynamics of this line quite a lot, so listen to the audio to capture the feel of the phrase and work out your fingering in advance before attempting it at speed.

In the hammer-on/pull-off phrase that starts this idea, I'm deliberately including an F note, which is the b9 of E7, for color. The rest of the lick comes from E Mixolydian, but I reference that F note briefly again toward the end.

In bar two, to play the string-skipped double-stop, hold down the top three strings at the 7th fret with the first finger. All the adjacent notes, not on the 7th fret, are played with the third and fourth fingers. You'll need to pluck or hybrid pick the first few notes. You can keep fretting in position at the 7th throughout this lick.

In bars 3-4, this scalic run uses B Mixolydian (B C# D# E F# G# A). Listen out for the changes of rhythm and "breaths" in this line.

Example 4e

For the turnaround section, we begin with a chromatic approach double-stop that targets the 3rd and 5th (C#, A#) of F#7. There are no big technical challenges in this lick but make sure you take the whole step bends to their full extent to hit the desired pitch.

Example 4f

We begin a new chorus of this blues with a new idea: using two different motifs to create a melodic theme. In the pickup bar and bars 1-2, the idea is expressed in question and answer format. In bars 3-4, a motif is played on the top two strings. Each statement of the idea begins the same way, but each ending is varied. This is a great way to develop new ideas if you're stuck for what to play. On the audio, you'll hear that I'm picking closer to the bridge when playing this motif to produce a brighter, more cutting tone.

Example 4g

Next up is an idea that utilizes different rhythms and picking approaches to create variety. Throughout bars 1-2 I'm picking more aggressively, a little towards the bridge for a biting tone. For the lick in the latter half of bar two, listen carefully to the audio to capture the feel of the 1/16th note triplets, as it's very hard to convey this in notation. The idea is that the line moves quite freely over the solid backing of drums and bass, to achieve a fluid, vocal sound. Take the same approach with the triplet-based licks in bars 3-4.

The next lick begins with a targeting idea that is simple to do but always effective. In the pickup bar, an ascending run leads to a blues curl bend on the second string that falls on the first beat of bar one. The A note is bent just shy of A#, which is the 3rd of the F#7 chord. Regardless of what you play around it, hitting a defining chord tone on the down beat always works to spell out the harmony and ground your ideas.

In bar two, this line is built from E Mixolydian, but to freshen things up I've made use of the top two strings played open at various points, both of which are scale tones. The use of the open high E string is practical here, as it enables the fast position change to hit the note at the 14th fret.

Bar four has a fast descending motif that repeats. Because it's a six-note phrase, it's another idea that would shift across the beat if we extended it over a few bars. The notes come from the B Blues scale (B D E F F# A) except the last note in the phrase (G#) which is borrowed from B Mixolydian. Because this lick is played over a B7 chord (B D# F# A), that G# strongly wants to resolve to either to an A (the b7) or root of B7.

Example 4i

Here's a challenging line for you to tackle that uses rhythmic variety and some irregular note groupings. In bar one, after the opening phrase, hit the high B note, and the open B string that follows, with plenty of attack and confidence. After playing the open string you'll immediately need to play the top string lick in bar two that follows on. Think of the open B as a springboard to launch the next part of the line.

In bar three, after the double-stop lick, a long line begins that lasts for the rest of this bar and bar four. I played what I felt in the moment and this is what came out! The result was a passage of 1/16th note triplets and then some odd note groupings. At the end of bar three, the group of seven notes is really an ascending run of eight straight 1/16th notes, but because of where I began the run, the eighth note in the sequence has spilled over into bar four. Listen to the audio and you'll hear this. As always, break down a long lick like this into more manageable chunks, working out the optimum fingering for each part, then connect the parts together.

Example 4j

Example 4k begins with another fluid line over the E7 chord. In the passage of 1/16th note triplets, I added in a couple of color tones to spice up the harmony, including a C note (the #5 of E7) and F# (the 9th). Visually, you can see from the notation that the simple theme I used throughout this lick was to keep repeating the B note on the second string 12th fret. It's the 5th of the E7 chord and obviously the root of the B7 chord and it glues this line together.

Example 4k

Here's the final example which completes this slow blues ballad in B. Expressive bends signify the turnaround changes in bars 1-2. Bar three begins to bring the energy down as the tune heads into its conclusion. In bar four a B9 chord is played which is approached from a half step above – an idea you'll have heard used before by many blues greats. Really pull back on the tempo here as the tune is about to end.

We close out the tune with a free time lick. For the pedal tone part of this lick at the end of bar four, it might help you to hold down a partial B7 chord shape in 7th position, though it can be played without.

Example 4l

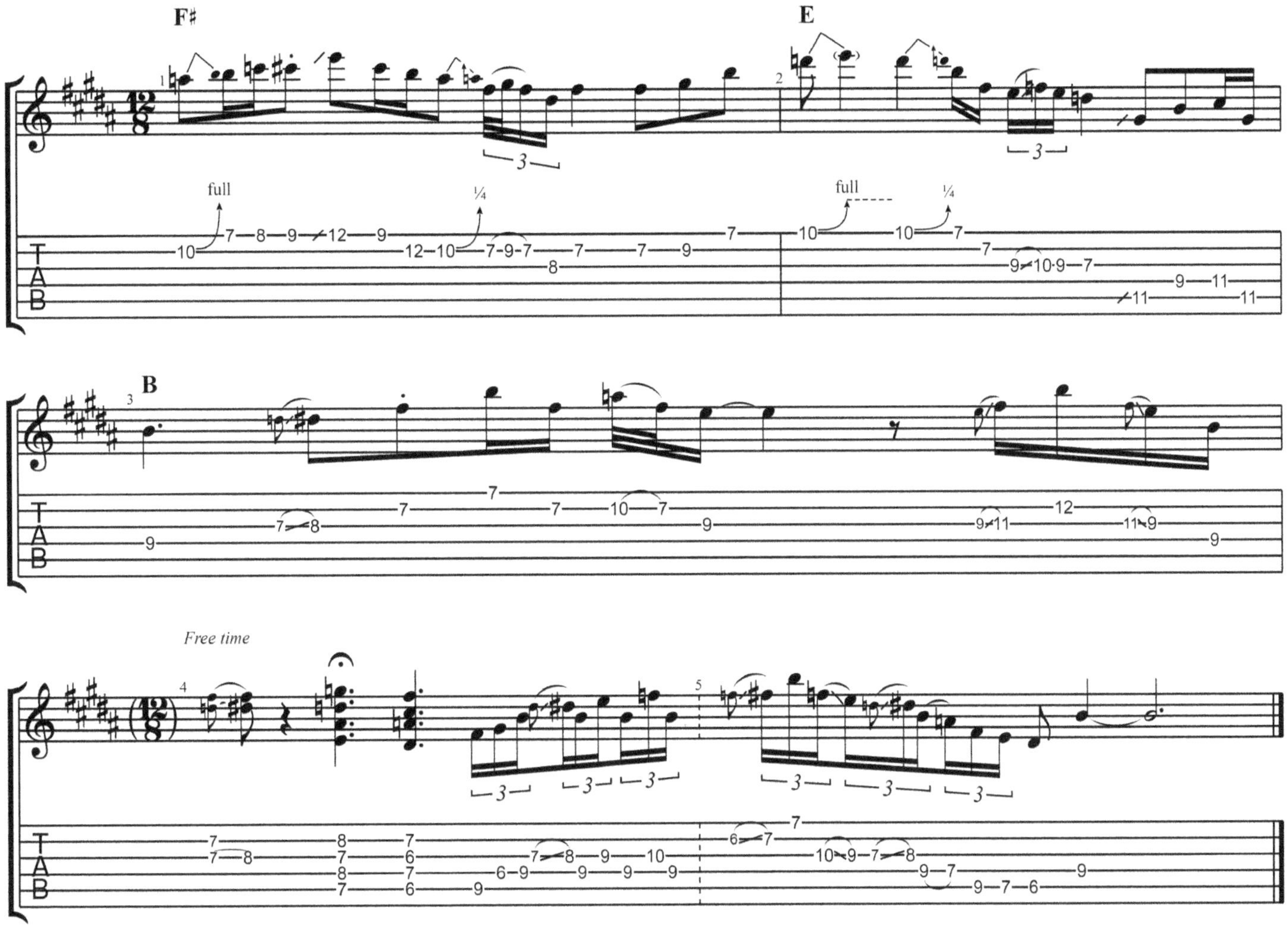

Chapter Five – Classic Rock Blues

The musical genre of Blues-Rock came to prominence in the late 1960s, combining the simple chord progressions of blues with the energy, volume and aggression of classic rock. It often focused on instrumental music, and during this time a number of classic bands emerged. Cream (with Eric Clapton), John Mayall and others came from the British blues tradition, while in the US, Paul Butterfield and Canned Heat were among blues-rock's earliest pioneers. Later, in the early 70s, musicians like Johnny Winter and the Allman Brothers took the genre into harder blues-rock territory.

In this chapter we're going to take a classic blues-rock progression, played in 6/8 time, and look at a collection of licks you can use to update this classic format with some modern blues ideas.

This time we are in the key of A Minor and the majority of the examples here are drawn from the A Minor (A B C D E F G), A Minor Pentatonic (A C D E G) and A Blues (A C D Eb E G) scales. These are the go-to scales players always turn to when faced with a tune like this, so the challenge for us is, how do we avoid playing too many clichéd ideas and make those routine scales sound fresh and exciting?

The answer is to apply the techniques we've been discussing. As well as focusing on expressive techniques that help us to get the most out of every single note, we'll look at lines played with odd note groupings, motif development, intervallic lines and some special hybrid-picked passages.

We begin with a question and answer line spread over eight bars. There are two question statements and two responses. The notes come the A Minor Pentatonic and A Blues scales.

We're aiming for an authentic vocal-like sound and that means injecting every bend and slide with attitude and emotion. You'll notice that the last note in the pickup bar and the first note of bar one are the same (A) but on adjacent strings. This is a common blues move and you can slide into the A on the second string if you like, to add to the vocal phrasing. When you play the "answer" phrase in bar two, keep this lick loose and fluid in its timing. The same applies to bars 6-7.

Example 5a

The next example begins by setting up a motif on the top two strings. Using whole step bends here helps to inject some emotion into the phrasing. The motif is developed further in bar four, before we move away from it in bar five. Notice here that initially I am restricting myself to a limited range of the fretboard.

In bar six, this slippery, rhythmically complex phrase uses a mixture of triplets to create a lick that slides between the b5 note of the A Blues scale (Eb) and other scale tones. The line is intended to "float" over the time of the backing so play it fairly loosely.

Example 5b

Example 5c is the turnaround part of the progression. In order to add some color to the potentially bland A Minor scale, in bar two I've added in some altered tones. First, the Bb note on the top string is the b9, then the Eb note on the third string is the b5 (which could also be seen as coming from the A Blues scale).

In bar six, this phrase is intended to be "stretched out" over the timing of the backing track for effect, so check out the audio reference and make sure to play the full note durations.

Example 5c

Next up is a motif-driven line to start the next chorus. There are a mixture of whole step bends and blues curls here, so look for accuracy in your pitching when moving between them. Aim to imitate vocal phrasing as much as possible with this line and notice where the "breaths" occur.

Example 5d

As you begin to build a solo, it's important to gradually ramp up the excitement. In this line that is achieved via two rhythmic motif licks. The first motif occurs in the latter half of bar one. It repeats immediately, with a slight modification, and so shifts to a different beat of the bar. It's repeated twice more, then at the end of bar three forms the start of the fast run of bar four.

Bar four's run is tricky to pull off, as are many licks that are played "in the moment". It's easier heard than read, so listen to the audio a few times to get the sense of how the lick works, then break it down into smaller groups of notes to work out a fingering that is comfortable for you.

At the end of bar five, a bit more color is added by bending to the 11th (D) of the Am chord. In bars 6-8, make the most of the slides between scale tones to add vocal phrasing.

Example 5e

The main idea of this example is another rhythmic motif, which begins partway through bar four.

Rhythmically, the lick begins with the last two notes of bar four, which are straight 1/16th notes – the second of which is bent slightly with a blues curl. This is followed by a 1/16th note triplet phrase, then two more straight 1/16ths to complete the seven-note phrase. Don't dwell on the bend too long or you'll lose the timing of the phrase – it should be executed with a slight push of the string to send it sharp.

Melodically, there is an emphasis throughout on the b5 tone (Eb) of the A Blues scale, and the seven-note phrase ends on a G note, the b7 of the A minor chord.

Play the phrase slowly to begin with to get it sounding smooth.

Example 5f

The next example really messes with the tempo! During the opening bars, for effect I'm deliberately playing more fragmented phrases and picking with a staccato approach to make the notes pop out. It's all done for dramatic effect.

In bars 3-6 we have some phrases that cut against the time feel of the track. In earlier chapters, we've encountered triplets being played over a straight 4/4 beat to create a "3 over 4" effect. Here I've reversed this idea to create a 4 over 3 feel. So, while the drummer is emphasizing the "1 2 3 4 5 6" swinging triplet groove, here we play straight 1/8th notes with a staccato attack.

Example 5g

The turnaround part of this chorus begins with a fast triplet-based lick. In bar one, the notes come from the A Blues scale that we've used extensively throughout these examples, but in bar two, over the D chord, we switch to the D Blues scale (D F G Ab A C) to create a contrast in color. It's the same idea we've explored before of treating each chord as its own tonal center and exploring the melodic options.

Example 5h

The next example brings together a focus on articulation and, later, hybrid picking. In the opening bars, I'm tremolo picking the notes for effect (rapid down-up alternate picking), before moving into a repeating phrase. In bars 5-8 the idea is to hybrid pick a string-skipped phrase that gradually gets wider and faster. It's hard to sensibly notate the super-fast ending of the lick, so you just need to listen to it to understand how it should sound.

The whole lick is made easier if you hold down a partial Am11 chord shape in 12th position and keep the E note on the fourth string 14th fret held down with the third finger for the duration of the lick.

Example 5i

The next example makes more use of double-stops to create a motif and punctuate the phrases. To add some drama, there is more tremolo picking in bars 4-5 and a quick hybrid picked string skipping lick. In bar seven we're playing with a 4 over 3 feel again.

Example 5j

In the next example, over the D chord in bars 1-2, I've changed up the scale approach again to create variety and introduce a surprise to the sound. Here, we're viewing the D chord as a V chord (D7) and using the D Mixolydian scale (D E F# G A B C) to form the melodic line.

In bar three, we change the scale again, this time to D Minor Pentatonic (D F G A C), and the fast run here is based around the familiar pentatonic box shape in 10th position. It's mainly hammer-ons and pull-offs and the challenge here is to make it sound smooth at tempo, with the hammered notes as loud as the picked notes.

The lick in bars 7-8 is best hybrid picked. It represents a bit of a fretting hand stretch to play the A note on the first string 5th fret with the first finger, and the second string 9th fret with the fourth finger, but this is the best approach to get the right sonic results, allowing the notes to ring into each other.

Example 5k

In this example I'm using double-stops to punch out a strong rhythmic phrase over the A minor section. It's a very simple device but can be really effective if used sparingly and in the right place, which here is at the climax of the solo.

The line ends with a repeating motif that highlights the b5 of the A Blues scale.

Example 51

The penultimate example repeats the chord progression of the previous example as a tag ending to the tune. In bar two the hybrid-picked lick has notes moving in contrary motion, ascending on the second string and descending on the fourth string, and this turns into a motif lick on the top strings. Barre your first finger at the 5th fret to play the beginning of this phrase.

In bar four, you'll recognize the shape of this lick, based around an A Minor Pentatonic box pattern in 5th position. In bar six, a 4 over 3 feel has the effect of slowing the lick down after the fast run of the previous bar.

Example 5m

And finally, a lick to end our blues-rock tune. It uses the A Minor Pentatonic and A Blues scales on the lower strings and slides between scale tones for articulation. Bringing the melody down onto the lower strings is a good way of signaling that a piece is coming to an end.

Example 5n

Conclusion

I hope you've enjoyed coming on this modern blues journey with me. So, where to from here? First of all, aim to develop your overall phrasing and solo storytelling by using the blues toolkit ideas discussed in the introduction. These are tried and tested techniques and will go a long way to improving your overall musicianship:

Feel and phrasing (inject your lines with emotion and get the most out of every note; play lines that cross the bar line and flow over the changes)

Storytelling devices (use call and response phrasing, repetition, and develop motifs and themes)

Country-Jazz influenced licks (experiment with chromatic passing notes and implied chord changes; aim to play more intervallic ideas at times)

Rhythmic variation (keep your lines rhythmically interesting, combining different note values, and always choose groove over clever note choices)

In your practice sessions, try my idea of restricting yourself to play a whole solo in a small zone of the neck (say three frets) or just using the top two strings, for example. There is freedom in limitation because it forces you to think more creatively and work harder to keep up the interest. This kind of restrictive playing will improve your phrasing almost immediately.

Lastly, try hybrid! I know hybrid picking is not for everyone, and this book certainly doesn't rely on it, but it revolutionized what I was able to play and opened up a whole vista of new ideas for me. Experiment with it and incorporate this technique into your playing if you can.

Good luck!

Josh.

Connect with Josh

Official website:

https://www.joshsmithguitar.com

Facebook:

https://www.facebook.com/joshsmithguitar/

Instagram:

https://www.instagram.com/joshsmithguitarzan/

YouTube:

https://www.youtube.com/user/JoshSmithGuitar

www.ingramcontent.com/pod-product-compliance
Lightning Source LLC
Chambersburg PA
CBHW081436090426
42740CB00017B/3333